AND PILATE ASKED...

W. A. POOVEY

AND PILATE ASKED...

SERMONS FOR LENT

AUGSBURG PUBLISHING HOUSE

Minneapolis Minnesota

AND PILATE ASKED

Library of Congress Catalog Card No. 65-12132

Acknowledgments are listed on page 93

Manufactured in the United States of America

Contents

Pilate entered the praetorium again and called Jesus, and said to him. "Are you the King of the Jews?" Jesus answered, "Do you say this of your own accord, or did others say it to you about me?" Pilate answered, "Am I a Jew? Your own nation and the chief priests have handed you over to me; *What have you done?*" Jesus answered, "My kingship is not of this world, if my kingship were of this world, my servants would fight, that I might not be handed over to the Jews; but my kingship is not from the world." Pilate said to him, "So you are a king?" Jesus answered, "You say that I am a king. For this I was born, and for this I have come into the world, to bear witness to the truth. Every one who is of the truth hears my voice." Pilate said to him, "What is truth?"

John 18:33-38

one • the question of guilt

What Have You Done?

There is a crash in the kitchen. Almost instinctively, the mother in the next room cries out, "What have you done?" A man running from a building at night is cornered by a policeman who demands: "What have you done?" A teenager calls his father to say he is at the police station. The first question is: "What have you done?" This is the question of guilt. It implies immediately that a breach of conduct has taken place. And the question carries the same implication when Pilate asks Jesus: "What have you done?"

Our first reaction is scorn and anger. How dare this Roman ask Jesus such an insulting question. Jesus has done nothing wrong. He has gone about the countryside healing the sick and teaching men wonderful truths about God. Proud Roman governor, you are not even worthy to wash this man's feet. "What have you done," indeed!

A second thought brings a different turn to this question. If we are honest, we will have to admit that by earthly standards Jesus has done much to arouse men's ire. He is guilty, guilty of revolutionary teaching that makes Marx and Lenin look like pikers. Because of his teachings, Jesus would have been condemned in any era of any country in the world. Men would always have occasion to ask him: "What have you done?"

Do these seem like wild words? Then I ask you to consider carefully with me this question of guilt. I think every Christian should be very clear about the disturbing nature of Jesus' work, for we are partners with him in that work when we bear his name. What did he do?

To begin with, *Jesus upset men's codes and standards!* To understand this, we must realize that every group of people living together in the world has some kind of standard or code by which it abides. The natives in New Guinea can perform certain acts, but other things are "tabu." In atheist Russia you do not find chaos, but a clearly defined code of conduct. Even that assembly of hoodlums, the Casa Nostra, has certain standards which are rigidly enforced. Every group demands certain actions from its members and commends those who abide by group-approved standards.

And Jesus Christ upset the applecart. He made it plain that man's ideas of right or wrong make no difference. He pointed out that whether or not our fellow men approve our actions is of no particular importance. It is God who judges and it is God who will judge. God's standards are the only ones that are important. God sees not only the outward act, but also the inward thought. Thus Jesus indicated that the sin of adultery is not only a sinful *act;* it also includes the lustful thought and the lustful look. Murder is not only the slaying of another human being, but the harboring of vengeful thoughts against our brother.

We sometimes wonder why Jesus spoke so harshly against the Pharisees of his day. But here is the explanation. They sought the praises of men; they were satisfied if they acted in accordance with their own approved standards. "Whitewashed tombs, full of dead men's bones," he called them, and though they recoiled from his attack, they could not deny the truth of his statements. But what a revolutionary thought—even the leading religious figures were evil because they lived by their own standards rather than by those of God.

Included in this earth-shaking teaching was the fact that men would be judged by God, according to God's standards, at the end of this life. No matter how pleased they might be with their own actions, no matter how much their friends and neighbors might commend them, the important thing was what God would think. And God would ask the question which Pilate asked: "What have you done?" Jesus never pictured God as Omar Khayyam did: "He's a Good Fellow, and 'twill all be well." Rather, God was pictured as one who has his own standards, and those set up by men have no validity before him.

It is hard to imagine a more revolutionary, more disturbing development than that which Jesus introduced. He upset man's whole moral code. He turned the prevailing standards of his world topsy-turvy. His enemies said, "He stirs up the people" (Luke 23:5), and he did precisely that. He was, and still is, guilty—guilty of teaching men that their own standards have no validity in the sight of God.

If you are a Christian, you share in this radical approach. For the Christian knows that it is God's standards which are important. He knows that only what is done for God will last. Of course, we do not offend our neighbors or disregard the laws of our nation. Indeed, the Christian wants men to see his good works and glorify God because of them. Nevertheless, the important thing for the believer is what God will think, not what his neighbor will say. Only when we have come to that conclusion have we really learned the revolutionary teachings of Jesus Christ.

But we have not yet exhausted the bill of particulars against Jesus. He had done something equally challenging. *He had exploded man's whole vision of progress.* He upset the approach of the human race to life in this world.

All human beings share a common belief in growth and progress—"getting somewhere" in this world. The goals may be different, but all men think that goals can be attained. The savage may have as his ambition more food or perhaps victory over his enemies in the neighboring tribe. The businessman may seek more business, more wealth. The student wants more knowledge or higher grades. The sick man wants to get well. Even people who dream of the past want progress by going back to what man once had, which naturally was better. Oliver Twist summed up man's attitude toward life when he asked for "more."

And Jesus exploded all of this philosophy of life shared by millions. He insisted that real progress is not made by the efforts of men, but by the power of God. Real progress comes only when man gives up striving for things of this world and puts God in charge of his life. So radical is this change that

Jesus described it as being *born again.* It can't be achieved by tinkering with our old nature. We must be given a new one.

How sweeping were Jesus' words when he proclaimed this truth! He pointed out that even if we possessed the whole world, even if our progress went that far, we would still profit nothing if our souls were to be lost. He said that a man would lose his life if he sought to save it. Only one who is willing to lose his life will find it. Indeed, from the very outset of his ministry, Jesus proclaimed this radical truth. With the words "Repent and believe" he called men to turn around, to reverse their direction in life and to follow him. His message always called for a radical change in men's hearts and in their ways of living.

The goals that men set for themselves never impressed Jesus. He didn't even own a house. When he died, his body was placed in a borrowed tomb. He pictured a rich man in hell and a beggar in heaven. Neither would Jesus be impressed by our modern life, with its gadgets, its luxuries, its ever-increasing knowledge about the world. For the Lord would know it to be an illusion. Real growth escapes us if there is no progress in the heart and life of a man.

When we look at life honestly, we must say that Jesus is right. We make progress and yet it doesn't bring the happiness we seek. When we manage to get rid of certain evils in civilization or in our own life, there is no real gain because the evil simply pops up some place else. John Wesley learned this, to his sorrow. In the course of his preaching about the sin of drunkenness, he managed to convince many to sign the temperance pledge. When they reformed, some of these men entered the business world and were so successful that they became completely wrapped up in their success. They had made no progress; they had simply exchanged one sin for another.

The truth is that mankind has been marching up a dead-end street almost from its beginnings on this earth. Only those who hear the call to turn around, to repent, make any real progress. The message of Jesus is clear—"seek first the kingdom of God and his righteousness." To the man with a large bank account, Jesus says, "What does it profit if you lose your own soul?" To the rulers of Russia who point to their material progress, Jesus says, "Man shall not live by bread alone." To the scientist, Jesus declares: "The fear of the Lord is the beginning of wisdom." Even to the doctors, with their wonderful gains in healing the body, Jesus brings the reminder that there can be no real soundness unless the soul has been healed.

In the opening scene of Bunyan's *Pilgrim's Prog-*

ress, Christian is seen fleeing from the City of Destruction. His friends and his neighbors try to restrain him. But he puts his fingers in his ears and cries out: "Life, life, eternal life." That's a picture of a man starting on the road to progress. For, as Jesus plainly indicated, there can be no gain in this life unless man first finds the new life in Christ.

Have you found it? If you are a Christian, then you are in agreement with the radical teaching of our Lord. You have learned to put God first. This does not mean you must sell all your property or spend all of your time reading the Bible. It means something deeper than that. It means that your goal in life is different from those of your fellow men. It means that you must plead guilty as Jesus had to plead guilty to the charge of upsetting the whole myth of human progress. For the Christian is one who believes that the power of the Holy Spirit must come first before the power of man can be exerted in the right direction. Have you adopted Jesus' radical approach? What have you done?

When the court indicts a man, it usually considers all his crimes. In keeping with this practice, we must add one more accusation against Jesus. He not only upset man's goals and his standards, but he also reversed the whole social scale. *He turned man's social standards upside down.*

All human beings have certain social standards.

Some professions are more honored than others. Some families have a more noteworthy history. Some possess more power and influence. Indeed, it seems that such social stratification is found even in the animal kingdom. Scientists have found that chickens have a certain pecking order. One chicken can peck another one, that one can peck someone down the list until you come to the bottom chicken who can't peck anyone. Human beings have their pecking order too.

Thus Pilate believed that because the Romans were a superior people, the Jews were dirt under his feet. The Jews felt they were a chosen race and had only contempt for a Roman like Pilate. In every succeeding age men have established some social standards. At times the most important man was the one with the fattest wife. Sometimes it was the number of children a man had, sometimes the "blue blood" in his veins. In our modern world we measure a man's standing by his wealth or his education. This is all a part of our human "pecking order."

When Jesus Christ came he changed everything. He made it plain that in the sight of God such human standards and ranks have no validity. Thus Nicodemus, though a ruler of the Jews, had to be saved in the same way as the Samaritan woman at the well. In God's kingdom, Pilate and the Jewish high priests had no more standing than the Galilean fishermen who followed Jesus. Indeed, when some of the Jews proudly proclaimed that they were Abraham's seed, which gave them special privileges, Jesus in no uncertain terms told them that since they were sinners, their ancestry made no difference. The words "no difference" run through the Christian message.

"No difference," for all have sinned. "No difference," for all can be saved by faith in Christ. The blue blood, the rich man, the important politician, and the lowest of the low must enter the kingdom in the same way. At the foot of the cross the ground is level.

But Jesus reversed the pattern, and this is a side of truth that we seldom hear about. Jesus pointed out that the more important we are in this world, the more difficult it is for us to become Christians. This doesn't mean God loves the lowly more than the important, but simply that the more important a man's position is in life, the harder it is for him to accept God's grace. If we have nothing, it is easier to rely on God's goodness. If we know little, it is easier to trust in God's promises.

That's why Jesus had to say that the publicans and the harlots would enter the kingdom of God before the Pharisees. That's why he indicated that it was hard for a rich man to be saved. Paul, commenting on this fact, declared that few wise and powerful men are called into God's kingdom. And in proof of this we are told that while the rulers refused to accept Jesus, the common people heard him gladly.

See how Jesus turns the whole social system upside down. He reminded men of the perils of position, of being at the top of the pecking order. Jesus doesn't shut the door in the face of the important, but he defines the nature of that door clearly. It is the same door as that used by everyone else.

Jesus' statement about the camel going through the eye of a needle has some bearing on this point. Jesus indicated that it was harder for a rich man to get into heaven than for a camel to get through the eye of a needle. Some have thought that there was a gate in Jerusalem's wall that was called "the needle's eye" because it was low and narrow. To get through this gate into the city, camels had to be unloaded and had to bend down. Probably this is not the correct explanation of Jesus' words, but it is a good description of what important people must do to become Christians. They must lay aside their baggage of wealth, fame, and titles so that they can enter God's kingdom on their knees just as all other men must do.

This reversal of the social scale is an important

truth for the Christian to observe. It should mean something especially in this Lenten season when we are to redouble our efforts to bring men to Christ. Often we pass by those who can be most easily won for the Gospel because we think they aren't important enough to bother with. And often we fail to realize that prominent and wealthy men face great difficulty when they wish to become Christians. We must be patient with them, but we must not falter in pointing out that there is no other door than that of repentance and faith if a man is to enter into the church.

"What have you done, Jesus?" The trial of Jesus should remind us that he was guilty. He had not done the things men accused him of, but he had turned the world upside down by shattering men's standards, their goals, their social pretensions. Gilbert K. Chesterton once said of Jesus: "There was a man who dwelt in the East centuries ago and now I cannot look at a sheep or a sparrow, a lily or a cornfield, a raven or a sunset, a vineyard, or a mountain without thinking of him." To those beautiful words we must add that we cannot look at the world of man without recognizing that Jesus has upset human society and has replaced the kingdom of men by the kingdom of God.

And as soon as it was morning the chief priests, with the elders and scribes, and the whole council held a consultation; and they bound Jesus and led him away and delivered him to Pilate. And Pilate asked him, "Are you the King of the Jews?" And he answered him, "You have said so." And the chief priests accused him of many things. And Pilate again asked him, "*Have you no answer to make?* See how many charges they bring against you." But Jesus made no further answer, so that Pilate wondered.

Mark 15:1-5

two • the question of bewilderment

Have You No Answer to Make?

A few years ago a man wrote a book about the silences of Jesus. I have never read it, but I'm sure that the book included *this* silence of our Lord as he stood before Pontius Pilate. This is one of the most significant and, at the same time, most baffling things that Jesus ever did. If that sounds like exaggeration, consider the situation. Jesus, on trial for his life, stands before the one man who can free him. His enemies are accusing him of all kinds of wrongdoing, and he knows that their accusations are false. Yet Jesus stands quietly, uttering not a word in his defense.

No wonder Pilate out of bewilderment asks the question that concerns us here. You can almost feel the baffled emotion in Pilate's voice as he says,

"Have you no answer to make?" Our sympathies are with the Roman governor at this point. For we, also, find it hard to understand this silence. Jesus had never been afraid of testifying before. He had spoken out bravely against his enemies and even against his friends when they were wrong. And now, at the crucial point, when the chips are down, Jesus stands silent. He has no answer to make.

We all feel that there was a purpose in this silence. We feel it has some real meaning. And yet what explanation can we give, particularly since Jesus himself refused to make any answer to Pilate's query? It seems that *there isn't any real and complete answer*. This silence of Jesus is connected with the whole mystery of the Passion history. When we begin to think of what happened to Jesus and of all the events of that terrible week, we simply must shake our heads and say, "Who can understand all of this?"

The silence of Jesus before Pilate is a part of the mystery of the crucifixion. Why did the Son of God have to suffer and die? How can the blood of this one save us? Indeed we must confess that this is a part of a greater mystery, God's whole mysterious plan of salvation. Consider his strange choice of Israel, rather than any other nation. Ask why he chose the time in history which he did as "the fullness of time." How did God guide the pattern of men's lives so that these two, Jesus and Pilate, stood face to face? When Good Friday was finished, Pilate probably said to himself, "I don't understand anything that happened today." And his bewilderment is ours too as we face the strange workings of God's mind.

God's mind—there lies the difficulty. We find it hard enough to determine what goes on in the mind of another human being. It is difficult to know why we do the things we do. It is harder still for someone else to explain our motives. We are convinced that certain people are extremely hard to understand. Men insist that they simply can't penetrate the feminine mind. Most Western nations are sure that the Russians are difficult to comprehend. So it goes.

But if men's minds baffle us, how then can we expect to understand the mind of God? Jesus himself reminded Nicodemus that if he couldn't explain how the wind blows, how could he expect to understand heavenly things. The wise men of this world have always acknowledged an area of truth where the human mind cannot penetrate. Job says of God: "Behold, I go forward, but he is not there; and backward, but I cannot perceive him" (Job 23:8). The Book of Isaiah declares: "Truly, thou art a God who hidest thyself" (Isa. 45:15). But perhaps Paul says it best of all. He writes: "How unsearchable are his [God's] judgments and how inscrutable his ways" (Rom. 11:33).

The church needs to take warning at this point, for the followers of Jesus Christ are often tempted to rush in and try to explain everything contained in the Word of God. We seem to feel that we are called upon to give an answer to every question which anyone can ask us. Sometimes the church fits the cruel description that one man made of another: "I wish I were as sure of anything in this life as he is of everything." Of course it is hard to say, "I don't know," but Paul reminds us that in this life we see "through a glass darkly." Even Jesus declared that there was something he did not know —the time of his return. Why should it be thought a disgrace to confess ignorance in certain areas of Christian truth?

Thank God we don't need all the answers. We may not know why Jesus stood silent before Pilate. We may not be able to explain all the workings of God's plan of salvation. But is Christianity a religion that supplies all the answers that the human intellect can demand? No! Christianity is faith in a person. It means that we know Jesus Christ as our Lord and Savior. This is the essential thing.

There is a silly story told about a young man who confessed to his girl friend that he couldn't understand how electricity worked. "It's simple," she said. "All you have to do is push a button and the light goes on." She didn't know much about electricity either—but she knew all that she needed to know. This is not a defense of ignorance. The Christian is not to remain a babe in the Word. He is to study and learn all that he can. Nevertheless, even if we must confess to ignorance at times, we can still know Jesus Christ as risen Lord and Savior. This is what enables us to be children of God. John Henry Newman, in his famous hymn, "Lead, kindly light," said it rather well. He wrote: "I do not ask to see the distant scene. One step enough for me."

However, we are not completely in the dark as to why Jesus stood before Pilate and refused to answer his accusers. We can give some partial reasons, even though we can't solve completely the mystery of the Passion. We find a clue in the exchange of remarks during Jesus' trial before the high priest. He was asked: "If you really are Christ, tell us!" He replied with these significant words: "If I tell you, you will never believe me, and if I ask you a question, you will not answer me" (Luke 22:67, Phillips Modern English).

With these words Jesus indicated that he had come to a point in his life where words were no longer of any use. If he did not die on this day, there would be another, for the rulers were bent on his destruction. This was not fatalism, but a realization on the part of Jesus that man's sinful nature would not be satisfied until the only perfect man who had ever lived had been destroyed. After all, if these leaders in Israel, representing, as they did, the highest level of religion in the ancient world, were bent on killing Jesus, what hope was there for mankind? Man's moral corruption, his inability to escape from his own weakness, his inability to rise above his baser self, was never more clearly demonstrated than in the trial of Jesus.

Thus the silence of our Lord before Pilate and his accusers is an eloquent silence. It says, "I know you, mankind. I know you are filled with evil and ugliness. The very presence of goodness is a reproach to you." The silence of Jesus tells us that our Lord was not surprised at the actions of Adolf Hitler. The terrible events that occurred in Nazi concentration camps did not shock him. He was neither amazed at the actions of Joseph Stalin nor at the things which atheistic Communism does today. The stories in the daily papers about murder and theft and rape are no surprise to him. He knows and has always known the truth about man. He knows that there is no one righteous, no not one.

And you and I need to pay attention to Jesus as he stands in silence. We need to face realistically what his silence reveals about man's innermost nature, for we are incurable optimists about human beings. We look at men on the surface and they seem pretty good, many of them at least. They do certain deeds of charity; they take on a veneer of honesty; even those who do not belong to the church behave in a fairly decent fashion. And so we conclude that human beings aren't really so bad. We are somehow like that man who jumped out of a tenth-story window. As he passed the fourth floor, he called out: "All right, so far." The top part may be fine, but when you get to the bottom, then comes the shock. Then evil and wickedness can be plainly seen.

This optimism explains why we are so shocked when sin shows its true nature. We are repelled by racial violence and wonder how it could have arisen. We are upset when a pillar of society collapses and proves to have been a crook and a scoundrel. We are even amazed at ourselves when we are swept into sin or when our anger flashes out of control. Let's take seriously this silence of Jesus and see how it witnesses against us and against all humanity. When Peter denied his Master we are told that Jesus looked at him. The heartbroken disciple went out and wept bitterly. As we see our Lord standing in silence before Pilate and realize how he is witnessing against man's sin, we too should be moved to repentance. We should call out: "God be merciful to me, a sinner."

Yet this would be a depressing thought if this were as far as we could penetrate into this strange silence. There is another partial answer that we can grasp if we understand this scene aright. The confrontation of Pilate and Jesus is a puzzlesome one by itself. But we cannot study this part of the story in isolation. The Passion of Jesus is one piece, not to be cut into little segments. And when we look at the entire story we are convinced of the fact that though the Jews plotted against Jesus and though Pilate condemned him to death, yet it was our Lord himself who willed to die. As he said, no man could take his life from him.

Consider the evidence. Jesus told his disciples before the crucifixion that he had to go to Jerusalem to suffer and die. Instead of staying out of that city where he knew death lurked, he set his face toward Jerusalem. Even in the upper room, when he knew who the traitor was and could have prevented him from acting, Jesus concealed his name from the other eleven and let him go so that he might do his nefarious work. And this silence before Pilate is just one more evidence that our Lord willed to die. When he could have pleaded for himself, he stood mute before his accusers.

Why? Because he knew man needed him. He knew that there had to be a sacrifice made for sin and he was that sacrifice. Jesus saw people wandering in this world as sheep without a shepherd. And he knew that the good shepherd is one who is willing to lay down his life for his sheep. The 53rd chapter of Isaiah pictures this silence of Jesus so well. "He was oppressed, and he was afflicted, yet he opened not his mouth; like a lamb that is led to the slaughter, and like a sheep that before its shearers is dumb, so he opened not his mouth" (Isa. 53:7).

This is the silence of love. Jesus knew that man would not believe in God's love if he simply talked about it. Man would scoff and declare that these were simply idle words. But you can't argue with a man who dies for you. You can't argue with a man who is willing to keep silent even when he knows that he can save his life by talking. The silence of Jesus speaks more eloquently of his love than all the words that he uttered while on this earth.

Suppose a young girl had a suitor with whom she flirted and talked, but wasn't sure about his love. Then suppose she fell into the lake and was in danger of being drowned. The young man responded to her call for help and rescued her at the risk of his own life. Do you think she would continue to ask, "Do you love me?" The evidence would be too plain for her to doubt. This is our situation in relationship to Jesus. He has proved and demonstrated his love. His silence before Pilate partakes of the very essence of the whole crucifixion. It is a part of the great drama of love.

We cannot grasp all the meaning of Jesus' actions. But we can see God's love shining behind the dark events of the crucifixion. Henry Webb Farrington, in his poem "Our Christ," sums up the position of man before his dying Lord:

I know not how that Calvary's cross
A world from sin could free:
I only know its matchless love
Has brought God's love to me.

This much we do know. And we can thank God for a Savior who stood in silence and refused to seek his own life at the cost of our own.

Then the whole company of them arose, and brought him before Pilate. And they began to accuse him, saying, "We found this man perverting our nation, and forbidding us to give tribute to Caesar, and saying that he himself is Christ a king." And Pilate asked him, *"Are you the King of the Jews?"* And he answered him, "You have said so." And Pilate said to the chief priests and the multitudes, "I find no crime in this man." But they were urgent, saying, "He stirs up the people, teaching throughout all Judea, from Galilee even to this place."

Luke 23:1-5

three • the question of identity

Are You the King of the Jews?

It has been said that one child can ask more questions than ten wise men can answer. Obviously there is no particular merit in asking difficult questions. Nevertheless, we have to take off our hats to Pontius Pilate. He was a pagan and a fool, but when Jesus stood before him, Pilate asked the right questions. Step by step, Pilate's questioning laid bare the whole nature of Jesus and the whole work of salvation. That is why, this Lenten season, I am seeking to spotlight a small segment of the Passion history. In this collection of sermons we are studying the wise questions asked by a foolish governor, not because the answers helped him but because here we may learn more about the one whom we call Lord and Savior.

The question here considered is the most basic of all. It is the question of identity. Who was this Jesus? Was he a martyr to his political views? Was he the victim of ecclesiastical plotting? Was he the uncrowned ruler of the land? Pilate wasted no time in posing the question of identity. "Are you the king of the Jews?" he asked. A little later he repeated the question: "So you are a king?" Pilate had to know. For the answer to this question determines all the other questions and answers.

You and I have to know the answer to this question too. If Jesus was simply a martyr to his views, we can pity him, but not worship him. If he was simply a great teacher who was destroyed by the enmity of his contemporaries, we can study his words, but we need not obey them. But if he was a king, if he was *the King,* then . . .

Suppose we borrow Pilate's tactics and begin with a statement as blunt as his question: *Jesus Christ is a king*. Indeed we believe he is King of kings and Lord of lords. He may appear weak today just as he did when he stood before Pilate. But we believe he is a king. The church of Jesus Christ is committed to that faith.

It is not hard to establish the fact of Jesus' kingship if we listen to the Word of God. Almost from the beginning of his life on this earth the word "king" was associated with him. When Jesus was born in Bethlehem, wise men came seeking him, saying, "Where is he that is born king of the Jews?" Very early in his ministry one of Jesus' disciples said of him: "You are the king of Israel." Jesus did not tell him: "Don't be foolish, Nathanael." Rather, he said, "You will see greater things than this." All of us are familiar with the events on Palm Sunday when Jesus entered the city of Jerusalem as a king might enter in triumph. The Gospel writers link this entry with the Old Testament prophecy: "Behold, thy king is coming." And as Jesus confronted Pilate, there is no evidence to show that he avoided or denied Pilate's question. The kingship of Jesus is plainly stated or implied again and again in the Gospels.

But the biblical witness is even more striking when we consider what a king is. I am not referring to those pale shadows of kingship that survive in the "constitutional monarchies" of Europe. A king in Jesus' day and in most of the history of mankind was someone who ruled, someone who gave orders and expected them to be obeyed. Louis XIV showed what a king was when he declared: "The state? I am the state." A certain African king once gave a graphic demonstration of the power of a king. In an effort to impress some visitors, the king ordered a company of his soldiers to march off a cliff. Obedient to his command, the soldiers to the last man marched to their deaths. Brutal? Yes, but a king is one who rules and commands.

From the very beginning Jesus possessed this power to command. He did not try to convince those four fishermen that they should become his disciples. He simply said, "Follow me." He did not tell Matthew the publican how great the advantages might be in becoming his disciple. He simply told him, "Follow me." When he taught the people, he taught them "as one having authority." Even the demons heard his command and obeyed him. There was never any of the beggar, the wheedler, the pleader, about Jesus. Like a king he gave commands and he expected them to be obeyed. He may have looked like a Galilean carpenter, but he spoke and acted as one born to the royal purple.

The answer to the question of identity is clear as far as Scripture is concerned. Jesus Christ was a king. He was the great king, our ruler and Lord. When we sing, "Crown him with many crowns," or "All hail the power of Jesus' name," we are testifying to the faith of the church. We are answering Pilate's question of identity with a positive testimony that the Christian church believes that Jesus is a king.

But having said that, we become involved in some powerful implications. If Jesus is a king, then those who dwell in his kingdom must be his obedient subjects. The kingship of Jesus implies his rulership and our willingness to obey. Heaven is not a democracy. Thus the Christian life means the yielding of our independence to the one who rules, to the one who is our king.

This isn't very popular. We want to be Christians, but we also want the right to make our own choices and to yield obedience only when it suits us. We would like to repudiate the atheism of William Henley and yet still echo his words:

I am the master of my fate;
I am the captain of my soul.

Several years ago I heard a prominent theologian objecting to the hymn "Have thine own way, Lord." He didn't like the line which says, "Thou art the potter, I am the clay." It seemed rather degrading to him to be regarded as a pot in the hands of a master potter. Most of us are probably inclined to agree with that viewpoint.

Yet, whether we like it or not, the minute we say that Jesus is a king, that Jesus is our king, we become like pots in the hands of a master potter. He rules and commands. We catch a glimpse of this in the Gospels when one of the disciples was bold enough to object to Jesus' going to Jerusalem to suffer and die. Did Jesus say, "Let's take a vote on it and decide what should be done"? He did not! He called that man a devil because of his well-meant advice. Jesus is a king, and you do not contradict kings.

Of course, this isn't the whole truth. There is such a thing as Christian freedom too. But the implications of Jesus' kingship are tremendous for you and me. They lay on our shoulders the burden of obedience. The Christian is a subject. He must hear the words of his Lord, "If you love me, keep my commandments." He must place himself under the dominance of a king. He is, as Paul declares, a slave for Christ's sake. The question of identity may seem an easy one for a Christian to answer, but it involves him in the necessity of obedience.

Moreover, there are implications here for the whole Christian church. The kingship of Christ reminds us that the church isn't an independent agency. It cannot act as it pleases or do what it wants to do. The church is under the necessity of obedience. Jesus told a bitter parable about some laborers who thought they could conduct the Lord's vineyard according to their own standards, but they received a rude and violent jolt and a hard reminder as to the identity of the true owner.

There are times when the church too needs a harsh reminder as to the nature of its head. There are those who think they can choose whether to do mission work or not. Some imagine that the church has the right to admit and exclude members on the basis of earthly standards. Recently a letter-writer to a national magazine insisted that the members of his church had built and paid for the building and that they would determine who came inside the door. If they chose to exclude certain races, that was their business.

But the true church of Jesus Christ has no such freedom. We serve under a king and we must do his will. How cleverly Paul puts this when he says that the church is the body of Christ. We like that description because it implies that we are connected to Christ. But it says more. It indicates that just as the head rules the body, so Christ rules his church. The church must also say, "Have thine own way, Lord, have thine own way."

The answer to the question of identity is a far-reaching one. We must agree that Jesus is king. But this king will rule. He will command and direct the lives of all who acknowledge his kingship. He is not just king of the Jews, but king of all who would follow him. The inscription over the cross said that Jesus was a king, but that may have been a bitter jest. You and I must say that he is our king, controlling and dominating our lives. This must be the inscription over our hearts.

But the word "king" has overtones and undertones. When we say it, we think of someone sitting on a throne. We hear the rustle of royal robes. We see the glitter of gold and the sparkle of diamonds. But Jesus stands clothed in a plain white robe. No retinue! No bowing courtiers! Pilate must have smiled a little when he said, "So you are a king?" Even today, when we are not used to royalty, the scene before Pilate seems a little strange. So we must add a word to our description of Jesus. He is not just a king. *He is a peculiar king*. He is like no other king that ever lived. Jesus himself makes this plain by declaring: "My kingship is not of this world." And it is only when we understand where the difference lies that we can properly answer the question of identity.

Notice how simply Jesus states the difference. "If my kingship were of this world, my servants would fight." In other words, Jesus' kingdom is not a kingdom of force, not a kingdom of violence. Men are not *compelled* to do his will in that kingdom. Earlier I mentioned the African king who ordered his soldiers to march off a cliff to their destruction. That illustration shows how earthly kings rule, but it doesn't tell us much about Jesus' kingdom. His is a peculiar kingship, a rulership of truth and love, not force.

If only the Christian church had learned that lesson from the beginning. It wasn't long after the church ceased to suffer martyrdom that it began to make martyrs of others. The history of the church in this world is stained with blood because it has forgotten the words of Jesus: "My kingship is not of this world." Even in our milder era, we are often not above using the methods of the world in trying to exalt Christ's kingship. When we pressure people into the church, when we seek to coax or wheedle or stir men by propaganda, we are forgetting the peculiar nature of our king.

Many a man is in the church only because he married a Christian woman and wants to keep peace in the family. Children often only wait until they can escape parental control to drop out of the church. The pressure of business, of social contacts, may force people into church membership against their wills. These are the methods of the world. Over against all such efforts to use force and pressure, our King says, "My kingship is not of this world."

The contrast between Jesus and Pilate also shows us the peculiar nature of Jesus' rule. Pilate is a governor, surrounded by every evidence of power and splendor. Jesus had to confess that he did not even have a place to lay his head when he was on this earth. The pomp and majesty of earthly kings are not a part of our Lord's rule. Simplicity, humbleness, and even apparent weakness characterize his rule.

This contrast between Jesus and the powers

of this earth has been repeated again and again in the history of the world. Paul must have seemed a poor figure in Ephesus as he preached in homes and in every place where he could gather a group of people to hear the Gospel. How much more magnificent was the temple of Diana of the Ephesians. Yet it was Paul who had the truth, and the followers of Diana who were deceived. I'm sure that Luther made a poor appearance at the Diet at Worms, in contrast to the brightly robed leaders of the church and the court. Yet it was Luther who was speaking the truth. Christ's kingdom is not one of pomp and splendor. He is a peculiar king.

And the church must realize the constant danger of the temptation to impress, to rely on outward trappings. We think we must have a finer building than the next congregation to impress men with our love for the Lord. Recently I saw a church advertisement which proudly proclaimed only one thing about the church—it was air-conditioned. Whether it preached the Gospel or not didn't seem important enough to mention. This desire to impress even invades the ministry. I know a pastor who loves to tell you how many Ph.D.'s he has in his membership, how many doctors and prominent citizens attend his church, as if this made it something special. And we Lutherans are fond of bragging about the number of Lutherans there are in the world, as if by counting noses we can impress other people. But Jesus is a peculiar king, and his kingship does not resort to earthly standards to gain its victory.

But the positive nature of Jesus' kingship is equally striking. He told Pilate: "For this I was born, and for this I have come into the world, to bear witness to the truth. Every one who is of the truth hears my voice." In other words, Jesus' kingship rests upon the power of truth. His kingdom is based on the proclamation of the Word. He conquers and rules, not by armies, not by force or pomp, but by the simple words of truth, by the simple preaching of the Gospel.

If ever there was a text that stresses the importance of preaching and witnessing, this is it. For this is how Jesus' kingdom is established and grows. Men hear the truth and are drawn to Christianity. This is the way Jesus conquers the hearts and minds of men—through the good news of the Gospel. Not by might, not by momentary impressions, but by the proclamation of truth are men saved and made subjects of this peculiar king. The church is sometimes tempted to try to use gimmicks and tricks to get men into God's kingdom. But all such efforts are in vain. The real power of Christ's kingdom is the power of the truth. Only through that can men's hearts be conquered.

I am reminded of what happened when the great preacher Spurgeon was asked: "Mr. Spurgeon, do you defend the Bible?"

"Defend it!" he replied. "I would as soon defend a lion. Let it out and it will defend itself." And so it will. The truth must be spoken. The word must be proclaimed. This is how Christ established and ruled his kingdom. Pilate may have thought Jesus was a peculiar king. So he is. But we must take him as we find him, for he rules in no other way.

Let us come back, then, to that strange meeting between a Roman governor and our Lord. Something wonderful should have happened when Pilate heard Jesus' words. He should have set aside the marks of his power. He should have knelt down before this one who was King and Lord. But he didn't do it. He did not listen to the answers to his own questions.

You and I dare not make the same mistake. We must bow before this Jesus. Each one of us must say, "Jesus is a king. He is a peculiar king. But above all, he is my king."

Pilate entered the praetorium again and called Jesus, and said to him, "Are you the King of the Jews?" Jesus answered, "Do you say this of your own accord, or did others say it to you about me?" Pilate answered, "*Am I a Jew?* Your own nation and the chief priests have handed you over to me; what have you done?" Jesus answered, "My kingship is not of this world; if my kingship were of this world, my servants would fight, that I might not be handed over to the Jews; but my kingship is not from the world." Pilate said to him, "So you are a king?" Jesus answered, "You say that I am a king. For this I was born, and for this I have come into the world, to bear witness to the truth. Every one who is of the truth hears my voice." Pilate said to him, "What is truth?"

John 18:33-38

four • the question of contempt

Am I a Jew?

"Am I a Jew?" This is a strange and yet enduring question. Pilate asked it over nineteen hundred years ago, and it could be asked today with precisely the same intonation and meaning. Perhaps nothing else testifies so eloquently to the continued existence of prejudice in this world as Pilate's question, "Am I a Jew?" The people in Shakespeare's day who rejoiced at Shylock's downfall would understand Pilate's query. The Nazis who broke windows in Jewish shops and finally destroyed lives in gas chambers would understand this question. Every man who feels contempt for another nationality, another race, would know the mood which prompted Pilate to ask: "Am I a Jew?"

How easy it would be at this point to begin to preach a sermon against race prejudice, to begin to talk about brotherhood and love for your fellow man. The presence of Jesus in the story makes the issue all the more striking, for certainly our Lord never taught hate or contempt for any man. In a day when the problem of race prejudice threatens to destroy this nation, the temptation is almost irresistible to cry out against the attitude of Pilate and by implication against the actions of all who seek to degrade and oppress their fellow men.

However, before we go too far, we must admit a very damaging thing. Pilate was right in his contempt. He had reason to be scornful of the Jews or at least of a good many of them. The Jewish leaders had caused Jesus to be brought before Pilate and, as Mark tells us, the Roman governor knew that they had acted out of envy. And despite his final failure to free Jesus, it must be admitted that Pilate did try almost every trick at his command to avoid condemning Jesus. It was not Pilate but the Jews who cried: "Crucify him. Crucify him." Thus the contempt in Pilate's voice was natural and understandable.

What we don't want to see is that in most instances of race prejudice there is some reason for contempt. The man who insists that Negroes are lazy and that they steal can undoubtedly point to examples of this very thing. The people who characterize Italians as gangsters can reel off an impressive list of names. The businessman who says that the Jew is money-mad and has no business ethics can generally quote chapter and verse to prove his point. Whether we speak of the French as immoral, the Germans as gluttons, Americans as sex-mad, or whatever our specific prejudice happens to be, there probably exists some basis for the accusation. Prejudice is not just ignorance, as many are inclined to think.

What is overlooked is that all we are establishing by such remarks is that man is sinful. Pilate proved it to himself; the Jews were envious and vicious. What he forgot was that he too was a sinner and that his shortcomings were no more acceptable to God than those of the Jews. Pilate was weak in the face of pressure, he was cruel in that he allowed an innocent man to be beaten, he was a murderer, since he allowed Jesus to be crucified although he knew there were no grounds for such an action. Yet he could say contemptuously, "Am I a Jew?"

This is the nature of all prejudice, of all intolerance. *It involves a denial of the equal guilt of all men before God.* It seeks to set up one set of weaknesses as being more acceptable than another. Prejudice says, in effect, What that man does is far more obnoxious than what I do. This is nonsense as far as God is concerned. Nowhere does God say that the weaknesses of one group of people are more tolerable than those of another. Indeed Paul, in writing to the church at Rome, implies the very opposite. He indicts the pagans and then turns sharply on his own people: "Therefore you have no excuse, O man, whoever you are, when you judge another; for in passing judgment upon him you condemn yourself, because you, the judge, are doing the very same thing" (Rom. 2:1).

It is important that we recognize this democracy of sin, this "we're all in this together" attitude of Scripture. Often, in an effort to be fair to those who are condemned, we run to the opposite extreme. The Jewish leaders have virtually been exonerated of crucifying Christ by many well-meaning people. If a Negro becomes violent and is involved in crime, we blame bad housing and practices of discrimination. If the Jew is greedy, we say that centuries of persecution have made him that way. If the Indian is lazy and drunken, we blame the white man. Doubtless there is some justification for such excuses, but let's not forget the simple fact of sin. No nation, no people, has a monopoly on either sin or virtue. The very presence of Jesus before Pilate testifies to man's involvement in sin, for otherwise there would be no need for a Savior. Neither the prejudiced man nor the unprejudiced one should forget the equal guilt of all men before God.

But we are fortunate that it was Jesus who stood before Pilate. For by his presence the Lord demolished once and for all the great fallacy of prejudice—*it ignores the individual.* Even if every Jew in Palestine had deserved Pilate's contempt, here stood one who did not deserve it. Jesus was a Jew, yet he was blameless. But the man who fills his heart with prejudice has no time for exceptions, no time to look into the individual heart. For prejudice is always the product of the lazy mind. It is much easier to characterize all Jews as sly and mean, all Irishmen as liars, all Negroes as thieves, etc., etc., than it is to look at the individual to see what kind of person he is. Pilate felt there was something a little different about Jesus, but his contempt for Jews included the man who stood before him.

A number of years ago, when immigration was causing America to have second thoughts about welcoming all people, Robert Haven Schauffler wrote a poem entitled: "Scum o' the Earth." The setting was Ellis Island, where immigrants once gathered before being granted admission into this country. These people were the "scum of the earth," but the poet pretends to see among them a sculptor like Praxiteles, a musician like Chopin, an explorer like Columbus, and finally a man with a face like that of the Christ. The rebuke to our prejudices was well put. The poem warns us against the error involved in Pilate's words, the error which would group all men in certain categories of nation or race.

One of the great truths of our Christian faith is the importance of the individual before God. Jesus' efforts to reach the woman at the well, the publican Zacchaeus, the fallen woman in Simon's house, show his concern for the individual. Indeed, his death on the cross was not a general amnesty, but an offer of forgiveness to each human soul who would accept it. Our Christian faith should remind us that we must have the same attitude toward others. Men must not be dealt with in bunches, like bananas. They must not simply be given certain scientific classifications, as is done for animals. Each man is a living soul, made in the image of God, and capable of having that image restored. To class him automatically with others because of the cut of his hair or the color of his skin is to deny everything that Jesus stood for. After all, the thief on the cross might have been regarded simply as one belonging to the class of thieves in the world. But to Jesus he was an individual in need of help, and he received that help.

Am I a Jew? The contempt in Pilate's voice was directed to Jews in general. It was an easy way to deal with Jesus and the Jewish leaders. But God does not deal with men that way. He is concerned with the human heart; he sees each man as an individual. It is interesting to note that the Book of Revelation speaks of names being written in heaven. A name is a personal, individual thing. It reminds the Christian of the lesson that Pilate forgot (or never knew)—men are individuals and must be treated as such.

No partiality! All of us probably agree that God doesn't show partiality toward any nation or people. That's why we can feel contempt for Pilate's contemptuous question: "Am I a Jew?" That's why we can smile at the egotism of an English admiral who once said: "God will not let his fellow countrymen down." We feel sure that God does not have any "fellow countrymen." Yet there is a sense in which God is partial or at least was partial for a long period in human history. For God did choose one people to be his people, one nation whom he protected and defended and kept alive through prosperity and adversity, captivity and military success. That nation was Israel. Strange that Pilate should speak words of contempt about the very people who never could be regarded with contempt. How fortunate it might have been for Pilate, had he been a Jew. But this proud governor *chose to ignore the special place of Israel in God's sight.*

We must add this tragedy to all the others that center around the crucifixion of Jesus. Jesus Christ, the explanation of the importance of the Jew, stood before Pilate, yet Pilate missed the point. Jesus was the reason for it all. The Jews had been delivered from Egypt and from Babylon so that Jesus might be born. The Jewish writers had penned the Old Testament so that it might speak about Jesus. The long struggle for Jerusalem, the terrible burden of exclusiveness, had been borne so that Jesus might come to deliver men from their sins. And now the final act of Israel's chosenness was taking place before Pilate's eyes. And he did not recognize it; he simply asked in contempt: "Am I a Jew?"

I wonder sometimes if we are not as blind as Pilate. For we too ignore the special place of Israel in God's sight. We forget the debt that every nation owes to Israel. No other people has been subjected to such continuous and bitter persecutions as Israel has suffered. The Negro has known only a short period of persecution as compared to the Jew. The "Dagoes," the "wops," and the "shanty Irish" have been fondly treated when one thinks of man's action against the Jew. Still today, in this land, there are places where the unwritten law says, "For Gentiles only."

Let me remind you that every book in the Bible, with the exception of the two written by Luke, was written by a Jew. All of the apostles, those men who made it possible for us to hear the Gospel, were Jews. Those grand figures that we study in Sunday school were all Jews. But above all, our Lord, who hung on a cross that you and I might be saved, was a Jew. The blood of Abraham and of David flowed in his veins. His language was the language of Palestine. His costumes and his customs were those of a Jew. You and I were saved by a Jew.

Isn't it time that we get the contemptuous tone out of our voice and thank God for the Jew? There might have been some justification for Pilate's attitude, though some of his countrymen had learned the truth about Israel, but there is no excuse for us. We can read the record and know what God did for us through his chosen people. Too often we allow ourselves to be poisoned by the actions of Caiaphas and Annas and forget that Calvary is not the story of what the Jews did to Jesus, but the story of what certain Jews did to another Jew. Even though Israel finally rejected the Messiah, that action should not be allowed to cancel out all that we owe these people for keeping alive the knowledge of the true God while our ancestors bowed down to idols or worse.

The story of Lent cannot but bring with it a reminder of the tragedy of the Jew. These people lost their favored position because they rejected their Messiah. But we have made it more difficult for them to be restored to an equal share in God's kingdom, for we have forgotten that our faith is founded on Israel and filled with Jewishness. The Nazis were consistent at this point at least. They saw that Christianity was bound up with the fact that God had chosen a people through whom a Savior should come. They tried to purge Christianity of all its Jewish features, but found that an impossible task.

Surely it is not asking too much that we seek to share with our Jewish brethren the blessings which they preserved for us. The story of Christ's crucifixion, far from filling our hearts with hatred against Israel, should remind us that only through Israel was salvation possible. Should we not extend a hand of love to the descendants of the apostles and of the family of our Lord himself? Harry Golden, that rather pungent Jewish writer, tells, in one of his essays, how frequently people try to convert him to Christianity. Then he complains rather plaintively that it is strange that people should want to spend all eternity with a man whom they wouldn't invite to have lunch with them. This is the tragedy of the Christian treatment of the Jews. Let's not make the mistake that Pilate did. Put away the contempt from your voice when you speak of those who were the people of the Lord.

No one can predict what the rising tide of racial hate will produce in our modern world. The contempt of Pilate has become the contempt of every people for those different from them. But at least let us who know better stand for love and brotherhood in the world today. The Christ who died for all men is offended if we limit his love by leaving out a single human being. John Oxenham has caught the true Christian spirit in his famous poem and hymn, "No East or West."

In Christ there is no East or West,
In him no South or North
But one great fellowship of love
Throughout the whole wide earth.

Join hands then, brothers of the faith,
Whate'er your race may be!—
Who serves my Father as a son
Is surely kin to me.

Pilate entered the praetorium again and called Jesus, and said to him, "Are you the King of the Jews?" Jesus answered, "Do you say this of your own accord, or did others say it to you about me?" Pilate answered, "Am I a Jew? Your own nation and the chief priests have handed you over to me; what have you done?" Jesus answered, "My kingship is not of this world; if my kingship were of this world, my servants would fight, that I might not be handed over to the Jews; but my kingship is not from the world." Pilate said to him, "So you are a king?" Jesus answered, "You say that I am a king. For this I was born, and for this I have come into the world, to bear witness to the truth. Every one who is of the truth hears my voice." Pilate said to him, "*What is truth?*"

John 18:33-38

five • the question of speculation

What Is Truth?

This is undoubtedly the most famous of the questions that Pilate asked Jesus. Few Christians remember his questions, "So you are a king, then?" or "What have you done?" But most of us are aware that somewhere in the interrogation of Jesus he was asked: "What is truth?" Somehow the words linger in our memory.

It is strange, however, that we should remember this question. After all, Pilate didn't expect an answer, for he turned on his heel and walked away. Moreover, centuries of probing have not furnished us with a clear idea of what Pilate meant by these words. Some have thought that the Roman governor had spent a long life of searching for truth and that in this question he is making a statement of his disillusionment. He is saying, "What is truth?

You can't find it anywhere." Others have felt that the words simply express a cynical attitude, saying in effect: "There's no use talking about truth because you can't find it anyway." Unfortunately, we don't have a recording of Pilate's voice; we can't decide his real meaning.

Why, then, should this be a famous question? Probably because it strikes a familiar and responsive chord in many hearts. Pilate was neither the first nor the last to ask: "What is truth?" The logic and the speculations of philosophers center around this particular question. The explorations of scientists finally boil down to a search for ultimate reality, a search for the truth behind the universe. And certainly those interested in religion have always been concerned about truth in one form or another. The great arguments by theologians generally deal with some phase of the question: "What is truth?"

It would be presumptuous to try in one sermon to answer this problem that men have explored through the ages. Nevertheless, if some answer is to be found, it should be discernible in this confrontation between Pilate and Jesus. Therefore I invite you to look carefully at this question, a question which may be called the question of speculation. For there is an air of unreality, of speculative philosophizing, about the statement: "What is truth?"

Let it be said at the outset that this air of speculation is a deceptive one. This is not really a question for speculation. Pilate treated the matter before him in this manner, but by so doing he was avoiding the very question which he had asked, "What is truth?" For truth as far as Pilate was concerned at that particular moment should have been to do what he had been sent to do, to act in the way he was supposed to act. He had been sent to Palestine to administer justice to the people of that land, including Jesus. Here was his opportunity to fulfill his duty. Truth was not something for him to speculate about. Truth meant action by Pilate, action designed to free Jesus from the charges leveled against him.

For this is the nature of truth. It is not a matter of speculation, of reasoning about various things. *Truth is doing the will of God at that peculiar moment.* Truth is the decision that a man has to make about every activity which he carries on in this life. Of course, truth includes some reasoning; it may even include some speculation. But these are only means to an end. Ultimately, truth has to be concerned with action, otherwise it is useless philosophizing and dreaming. This fact is reflected on every page of Scripture.

Think of the man who came to Jesus at night and wanted to talk about religious matters. What was truth for Nicodemus, a speculation as to whether Jesus was the Messiah or not? No! Truth meant that Nicodemus needed to be born again and that he needed to make plain to the people of Jerusalem his intention to follow the teachings of Christ.

What was truth for the Apostle Paul? Was it the decision that he had been wrong in persecuting the Christians? That decision had to be made, of course, but ultimately truth demanded that Paul go out and spread abroad the good news of the Gospel.

Even in the Garden of Eden this same note appears. What was truth for Eve? Was it speculation about whether or not she would become wiser if she ate the fruit? No. Truth consisted in being obedient to God's command, doing the thing which God had told her to do, resisting the temptation that was set before her. This is always truth—the decision to do the will of God at that particular moment.

It's not hard to see what truth means for us as individuals. If a man is a businessman, truth means being honest with his employees and his customers. Truth for a housewife means being faithful to her husband and being concerned for the welfare of her children. Truth for the student means being diligent in his studies and availing himself of the opportunities for learning that are available. Truth for the laborer means an honest day's work for an honest day's wages. Truth is always action, decision, doing.

There is a good example of the nature of truth in the Old Testament. Joshua, the great military leader of Israel, gathered all the people at Shechem and recounted for them what God had done for them. He talked about the false gods, whom some of the Israelites had served in the past, but he didn't engage in speculation as to who was the true God. He simply put the question to the people, ". . . choose this day whom you will serve" (Josh. 24:15b). This is truth—to decide, to act, to make a choice.

But we dare not overlook the appeal of speculation. Whether we like it or not, men like to reason and argue about truth. And it should be obvious why this is so. It's so much easier to speculate, to reason and argue. It's easier to think of truth as something in a book, something in a creed. As long as we can deal in those terms, we don't have to do anything. One of the prize examples of this was the woman at the well in Samaria. She may have been uneducated in many ways, but she knew all the tricks of human logic. She wanted to discuss the proper place of worship, whether it was to be Jerusalem or the mount in Samaria. This would be a nice religious argument and would avoid any mention of her immoral life.

The friends of Job were also good at playing this game. They came to see Job when he was at the bottom of the ladder, so to speak. But nobody said, "Here, Job, here's five dollars. Go out and buy yourself some clothes." Nobody suggested: "I'd better call a doctor and see if he can help you with those boils." These "friends" simply sat and talked. They speculated about whether or not Job was a sinner. But there was no action; it is always easier to talk than to act.

Men have played this game in every age. It's easy to talk about religion. It's easy to be concerned about right and wrong if we don't have to do anything. Think how we like to talk about the racial issue. If you want to get a group of people together, announce a conference on race and they will come from all parts of the country. But how slow we are to take positive steps to implement the results of the talking.

Think how in our modern world we like to speak about the ecumenical movement. We like to talk about how much we love our brethren of other denominations. We may even pass resolutions to that effect. But when it comes to positive, concrete action, we aren't quite ready to take any forward step. It is pleasant to think of truth in terms of words; it becomes something else when deeds are demanded.

Is there any real truth then? Of course there is. Pilate saw it clearly. He even began to carry it out as he tried to free Jesus; but it didn't take long before the spineless Roman governor had wavered and retreated. But truth was there. Pilate was called to do God's will. You and I are in the same position. We come to the fork in the road over and over again, and it doesn't do any good to stand and talk about what a nice road it is. If we want to go anywhere, we must decide. For that is what truth is—decision to do God's will in this life. Truth is action, not speculation.

Some of you may be wondering if this isn't a form of religious anarchy. Are we to go back to the days in Israel when every man did what was right in his own sight? Is truth a relative thing, a "sometime" thing? Are we to join in the chorus of the Mikado: "And I am right and you are right and all is right as right can be"?

To anwer this, we must look at the one who stands before Pilate. What did he say to provoke Pilate's scornful question: "What is truth?" In clear tones Jesus had stated his position: "For this I was born and for this I have come into the world, to bear witness to the truth. Every one who is of the truth hears my voice." How clearly Jesus says it. Truth is not simply action, blind action. *Truth is action based on acceptance.* And that acceptance means the acknowledgment of the lordship of Christ; it means knowing him as the divine messenger, the revealer from God, the Savior of mankind. After all, Jesus had said, "I am the way, the *truth*, and the life." He had declared that he was the light of the world. He had insisted that he was the door, the vine, the bread of life. Jesus is God's revelation of truth to the world, and there is no speculation required here, but only acceptance of a person.

Here is the source of all truth, the explanation for all existence, the meaning for every life. Truth stood before Pilate in the person of the Son of God, but Pilate was too blind to see it. Truth always confronts us in the person of Jesus Christ. He shows us what we are—weak and sinful. He shows us what we can become—forgiven and righteous. There is no need for speculation here, no searching after obscure meanings. Jesus Christ is God's message of truth to men and he confronts us in an effort to bring us to the truth. Pilate's question should not have been: "What is truth?" but "Who is truth?" The answer to that question, Jesus Christ, stood in his presence. Truth is to be found nowhere else.

This does not mean that men cannot *learn truths* without Jesus. An atheistic doctor may cure you of your aches and pains. An agnostic astronomer may be able to determine the movement of heavenly bodies. A religious heretic may make a discovery in the field of archeology that will prove a blessing for all true Christians. But when you get down to the core of life, to the real purpose and meaning of existence, then there is only one source of truth—Jesus Christ.

Pilate had the truth right before him. He had the answer to the age-old question, "What is truth?" But he missed his chance because he chose to put Jesus on a level with all other human beings. He saw Jesus as just another Jew, just another human being. And that viewpoint can never lead to real truth. There must be acceptance of the claims of Jesus, or disaster follows.

Indeed, what was said at the outset can be terribly misleading without this second understanding of the nature of truth. Truth is action, but unless there is also confrontation and acceptance of Christ, the result is disastrous. Napoleon had some wonderful ideas. Hitler had some high-sounding goals. But though they were men of action, they lacked the guidance of the real source of truth and thus plunged themselves and the world into disaster. And every life that acts must have the guidance of Jesus Christ.

Indeed, without that guidance it would have been better merely to engage in speculation. Pilate could have prevented much wrong if he had simply continued to talk. As long as he had not acknowledged the source of real truth, he was better off doing nothing. For the man without divine wisdom is like a surveyor trying to measure one hundred yards due north. If he makes a mistake and heads his instrument north-northwest, every inch he measures is a little farther from the real line that he wanted to stake out. If there is no real truth in a man's heart, every action drives him a little farther away from God.

There is but one way that men can serve truth in this life. There must be commitment, surrender, acceptance of the claims of Jesus. A simple example may show this.

A certain boat was known for the clumsy way it always docked. Men called it "Old Bust 'em up." One day the boat sailed into the harbor and docked as neatly as a new steamer. Somebody called out: "What happened to that boat?" "Nothing," came the reply. "We got a new skipper aboard."

That's the way it must be. For truth is action, but there must be the right skipper in charge. Man cannot simply speculate, as did Pilate. Neither can he act without knowledge, as Pilate also did. Man needs Jesus in his heart and a firm hand at the wheel, acting, moving, going forward in this life.

The poet Whittier once wrote:

For of all sad words of tongue or pen
The saddest are these: It might have been.

Those words could have been written for Pontius Pilate. He had the truth before him and he lost it. But we have the same opportunity, for truth is here before us. Jesus Christ wishes to come in and take charge of our lives. Perhaps he has done it before, but he would do so now in still greater measure. If we would know the truth, if we would live the truth, we must open our hearts to him; and then we must live and walk in the truth.

So Jesus came out, wearing the crown of thorns and the purple robe. Pilate said to them, "Here is the man!" When the chief priests and the officers saw him, they cried out, "Crucify him, crucify him!" Pilate said to them, "Take him yourselves and crucify him, for I find no crime in him." The Jews answered him, "We have a law, and by that law he ought to die, because he has made himself the Son of God." When Pilate heard these words, he was the more afraid; he entered the praetorium again and said to Jesus, "*Where are you from?*" But Jesus gave no answer. Pilate therefore said to him, "You will not speak to me? Do you not know that I have power to release you, and power to crucify you?" Jesus answered him, "You would have no power over me unless it had been given you from above; therefore he who delivered me to you has the greater sin."

John 19:5-11

six • the question of origin

Where Are You From?

There is a mystery about Jesus of Nazareth, a mystery that every generation of human beings has had to face. The problem is this—his accomplishments seem so far beyond his person. Consider the situation. As far as we can see, Jesus was a Jewish rabbi, a teacher. He lived some thirty-three years on this earth. On two occasions only, he went beyond the borders of Palestine and then only for a short distance. He never wrote a book. He held no political or ecclesiastical office. As far as we know, his contemporaries did not think him important enough to record his name in a book. Yet the whole modern world has been influenced by Jesus of Nazareth. There is probably not a single human being alive who has not in some way felt the influence of this Galilean rabbi.

This is the mystery, the mystery of the person of Jesus. Who was he that he could leave such an imprint on human history? Even the people in Jesus' day felt this aura of the unknown about him. Peter once said: "Depart from me, for I am a sinful man," and that's a strange thing to say to another human being. Some of the other disciples voiced the query when Jesus calmed a storm: "Who is this that even the wind and the waves obey him?" Even the officers who were sent to arrest Jesus insisted: "No man ever spoke like this man." Pilate, too, became engrossed in the mystery when he faced Jesus. With his uncanny ability to ask the right question, he inquired, "Where are you from?" This is the question of origin. It is close to the question of kingship, but it pushes the question back a step. "Where are you from?"

I do not propose to answer that question—not in so many words, at least. I simply want to lay the facts before you. If you are not sure of the answer, see if you can find that assurance. If you do know the answer to the question of origin, it will be helpful to review the facts and take another careful look at Jesus of Nazareth, who died on a cross.

Suppose we begin with a simple, four-letter word, "*love*." This is a familiar word to all of us, for we use it in many ways. We speak about "love" in terms of sex, in terms of affection, and in terms of understanding. But when we begin to think of love in connection with Jesus, then the picture changes. For *Jesus had a love that was beyond this world*. His love was not like ours: It ran with eagerness where our love stumbles lamely or refuses to go. Take a look at some of the people that Jesus met and you will understand what I mean.

If a man were to pick out the lowest level of society among the Jews, he would probably select the lepers. These poor people were outcasts who had to cry out, "Unclean, unclean" when they walked through the countryside. Men feared them and refused to come close to them. But Jesus came close to them. He touched them. He healed them. He forgave their sins, for his love included even the lepers.

Perhaps the next level would be the "fallen women" of that day. Man always ruins and then condemns—not the Master, however. He refused to condemn the woman who washed his feet with her tears and dried them with her hair, even though the pious Pharisee Simon thought she should have been sent away. Jesus talked to the woman at the well, knowing that she had had five husbands and was now living with a sixth, whom she had not even bothered to marry. Probably she came to the well alone because none of the women in the village would associate with her. But Jesus reached out the hand of love to her and made her one of his followers.

It would be possible to extend this list to great lengths. Jesus loved the publicans and Samaritans even though men considered them the offscouring of humanity. His love penetrated where even our interest would not go. Luther is reputed to have said: "Our Lord must be a pious man to be able to love rascals. I cannot do it and I am a rascal myself." But this love which is beyond this world showed itself most plainly at Calvary, where Jesus prayed for those who nailed him to the cross. Even a poor thief who cried out for help felt the encompassing power of Jesus' love. Truly this was a love unlike ours, unlike earthly love, for it reached out to those who were seemingly of no value but who still could respond to love.

Gilbert K. Chesterton, in one of his detective stories, distinguished the two kinds of love that are to be found in this world. One of the characters says, "There's a limit to human charity."

"There is," says Father Brown, "and that is the real difference between human charity and Christian charity. . . . It seems to me that you only pardon the sins that you don't really think sinful. You only forgive criminals when they commit what you don't regard as crimes but rather as conventions. You forgive because there isn't anything to be forgiven."

I think we must plead guilty to this indictment. But Jesus' love goes beyond that. It is a love which goes beyond this world. It is a love which still embraces the fallen, the outcast, the roué. Christ Jesus loved the pirates that fought on the seven seas. He loved the vandals who destroyed the Roman empire. He died on a cross of love so that every drunken bum, every thief, every murderer might be forgiven for his sin. Isaac Watts caught the wonder of this when he wrote:

Was it for crimes that I have done
He groaned upon the tree?
Amazing pity, grace unknown
And love beyond degree.

Where was he from? Was he purely a creature of this earth, simply a carpenter from Nazareth? Where did he get this love which goes beyond this world? I ask you to decide that question in your hearts.

But before you do, let's take a look at another simple word—"life." Of course, that is a big subject, so let us concentrate on the imperfections of our earthly existence. It's not hard to see them, for man is always striving toward a goal and never reaching it. Somehow we all make blots on the pages. Whether we talk about sins or failures or imperfections, the meaning is the same. Paul spoke for all humanity when he confessed that he didn't do the things that he wanted to do, but the things that he didn't want to do, he kept on doing.

But look at the life of Jesus. Here the picture is different. Here is *a life that is beyond this world,* for the shortcomings which we experience are not to be found in the story of Jesus. His life was like the seamless robe that he wore; there were no flaws, no imperfections in it. Thus Pilate had to confess: "I find no fault in him." Jesus himself could challenge his enemies with the words: "Which of you convicts me of sin?" The Word of God tells us that God made him *who knew no sin* to be sin on our behalf. Again we are reminded that although he was tempted as we are, Jesus remained without sin. Here is the sharp contrast between Jesus and every other human being. Here is the life that was beyond this world.

Perhaps a story will make the meaning clear. Two men were sitting on a train discussing the Christian church. They were exposing all its flaws, criticizing all its members. Finally a man behind them could stand it no longer. He interrupted the speakers with the words: "I have been a member of a church for many years, and I think I could add to your list of weaknesses possessed by Christian people. But think for a moment of Jesus Christ.

say a word against him." The men on the train were silent, for there was nothing to be said.

When you look at the records of other men, other great leaders, you will find spots in their lives. Socrates, Mohammed, Luther, Loyola—fill in the blanks yourselves, but always the story is a mixture of good and evil. Only one man remains untouched. Sometimes I think this is the real meaning of the transfiguration. It was not just the divinity of Jesus which shone on the mountain, but his holiness, his sinlessness. He lived a life beyond this world.

Who was he? Where did he come from? What is the answer to Pilate's question of origin? You must decide.

But perhaps we should see one more aspect of the life of Jesus. He was not just a pale, plaster saint. Jesus was a man who acted, a man who did things. And when you look at his record of achievement, you are forced to concede that he also had a *power beyond this world*. Immediately you think of miracles; certainly the miracles of Jesus were demonstrations of his power. The people who knew him, who saw him, believed that he had power to heal them and to bless them. His enemies did not deny his actions, they only declared that he did these things by Satan's power. Nevertheless, when we speak of Jesus' power which goes beyond this world, we mean something more than physical miracles. The real demonstrations of power were the instances of changed lives.

Think of that man Zacchaeus who climbed a tree to watch Jesus as he passed by. Zacchaeus was a crook and a robber, yet Jesus changed him into a God-fearing man who agreed to restore his ill-gotten gains fourfold and to give one-half of his goods to the poor. What a power to change and transform a human life! Or think of Nicodemus who came to Jesus by night and seemingly was unaffected at first; yet he came forth publicy at the crucifixion and showed that something had happened in his life on the night that he met Jesus.

There was a man who hated Jesus Christ, who even persecuted the members of the church; yet that man became the greatest Christian of all. What a power Jesus had, to touch and transform the heart of Paul. Every Christian who has felt the power of God in his life will testify that this Jesus has a power which is beyond this world.

I can remember a speaker from my student days in the seminary who made a profound impression on me. This man told the story of his life of crime. He declared: "Name it and I've done it." He was under sentence of death when the Gospel came to him and changed his heart. Later he was allowed to live and was finally freed. He spent his time telling others what Jesus Christ had done for him. That story could be duplicated in part by hundreds of people. I knew a woman who was so bitter because of the death of a child that she thought of self-destruction. Nothing kept her from that except the power of Jesus Christ.

We could go on, for the list is as long as the roll of the Christian church. Doctors have given up, psychiatrists have abandoned the case, parents have lectured their children, wives have pleaded with their husbands, and nothing has happened. But with the coming of the Gospel into a life there comes a change. This is the power of Jesus, a power that goes beyond anything man knows in this world. An old revival hymn puts it rather clearly.

I was sinking deep in sin,
Far from the peaceful shore,
Very deeply stained within,
Sinking to rise no more.

Love lifted me. Love lifted me.
When nothing else could help,
Love lifted me.

Love lifted. This is the power of Jesus. It is the power that goes beyond this world. And it forces us to face Pilate's question. Who is this one who has such power? Where did he come from? How could a mere man have such power, such love, such life as Jesus had? Is he merely a religious genius? Or is there more? Is he what he said and what others said about him—the Son of God? I place the decision in your hands. Pilate didn't learn the answer. Do you know it?

A sermon should end with an appeal and a plea. This sermon should end with the urgent demand that you yield your hearts to Jesus, that you open up your life day by day to his love and his goodness and his power. But I don't intend such an ending. Let me simply remind you that there was a man who thought for a time that Jesus had been a failure. He was a doubter, a man who wasn't sure whether he could continue his allegiance to Jesus. And then there came a day when this man Thomas fell down before his Lord and said, "My Lord and my God." Do those words suggest anything to you?

So Jesus came out, wearing the crown of thorns and the purple robe. Pilate said to them, "Here is the man!" When the chief priests and the officers saw him, they cried out, "Crucify him, crucify him!" Pilate said to them, "Take him yourselves and crucify him, for I find no crime in him." The Jews answered him, "We have a law, and by that law he ought to die, because he has made himself the Son of God." When Pilate heard these words, he was the more afraid; he entered the praetorium again and said to Jesus, "Where are you from?" But Jesus gave no answer. Pilate therefore said to him, "You will not speak to me? *Do you not know that I have power to release you,* and power to crucify you?" Jesus answered him, "You would have no power over me unless it had been given you from above; therefore he who delivered me to you has the greater sin."

John 19:5-11

seven • the question of power

Do You Not Know That I Have Power to Release You?

"Render to Caesar the things that are Caesar's and to God the things that are God's." Most Christians are familiar with this statement by Jesus. It seems to wrap up all the problems of church and state in a nice, neat little package. It says there is a realm for Caesar and a realm for God, and never the twain shall meet. But Jesus was fully aware that this was not a definitive statement. He knew that the line between these two realms is not as sharply drawn as one might think. And he was particularly aware that Caesar always wants to go beyond the power which God grants him. Government wants power over the church, yes, even over God himself.

Pilate states the proposition baldly: "Don't you know that I have power to crucify you and power to release you?" With that sweeping statement he seems to sum up plainly the age-old battle between religion and government. Hitler would have applauded this claim. Joseph Stalin would have nodded his head in agreement. And even some people in our land would be in agreement with the arrogance of the Roman governor.

Therefore it is very fitting, as we come to the close of these Lenten sermons, that we deal with what is the ultimate question in many ways. It is the question of who has the power. Who rules in this world—God or Caesar? Who rules—Pilate or Jesus?

Our first impulse is to say that this is a foolish question. God rules, of course. He is the Creator, while man is merely the creature made by God's hand. When we think of this question, our minds may roam back to that magnificent fortieth chapter of Isaiah where men are pictured as being like grasshoppers in God's hand and the nations like a drop in a bucket. Isaiah's words are very reassuring for any Christian who fears the power of government.

However, when we abandon the poetry and look carefully at the *events* of Scripture, we must confess that the power seems to lie in the hands of Pilate, the hands of Caesar. After all, there were three crosses on Golgotha, not two, and the third cross testifies that Pilate was not boasting when he declared that he had power to crucify Jesus.

Moreover, the story of Jesus cannot be regarded as an exception to the rule. True, Jesus was willing to suffer and die for men's sins, and yet he was just the first of a long line of Christian martyrs throughout history. The traditions of the church indicate that only one disciple (and possibly not even one) died a natural death. The others suffered and died for their faith. Indeed, whenever government has chosen to use its power, it has had no difficulty in dealing with the children of God. Where was God when old Bishop Polycarp was burned? Where was God when Nero persecuted the Christians of his day? And lest we think of all this as ancient history, we need to be reminded that the twentieth century has seen more religious martyrs than the preceding nineteen centuries of the Christian era combined.

The power always seems to be in the hands of Caesar. Pilate made no idle boast when he declared his power; the forces of government possess the verdict of life or death over God's children. The cross of Christ is not only a symbol of redemption, but also a picture of the power that Caesar possesses when he strikes against God. The history of man shows that men die because they are true believers and God doesn't prevent it.

Many of us may be moved to share the sentiment of A. E. Housman in his poem entitled "Easter Hymn." In the first verse the poet comments that if Jesus is still in the tomb, let him rest in peace. But then comes the second verse:

But if, the grave rent and the stone rolled by,
At the right hand of majesty on high
You sit, and sitting so remember yet
Your tears, your agony and bloody sweat,
Your cross and passion and the life you gave,
Bow hither out of heaven and see and save.

But Jesus does not do it. He doesn't come down from heaven to rescue his followers. Men look at the world and they see that the power is in the hands of Caesar. His hand seems more powerful than God's hand. The cross itself is a witness to the strength of the forces of darkness in this world, a witness to the fact that Caesar can defy God.

But before we throw in the sponge, let's take another look at this meeting between Christ and Pilate. Suppose for a moment that God had determined to rescue Jesus and thus make plain to Pilate that he didn't possess the power he claimed. Suppose that the twelve legions of angels that Jesus claimed would fight for him had actually done it. It would have been a magnificent scene, of course—divine dive-bombers swooping low, heavenly helicopters snatching Jesus from the control of Pilate. Or suppose that when men challenged Jesus to come down from the cross he had done so, calmly releasing himself, and proving that Pilate wasn't able to crucify him. What then?

It would have been a stunning thing. Everybody would have been duly impressed. But would God's purposes have been accomplished? Would anybody have become a new man in Christ because such a miracle had occurred? Quite the contrary. God would merely have revealed that he had more power than Pilate. God would have been proved stronger, but no different. Admittedly that's the picture that many people have of God. He is a kind of superman. He can perform miracles and force men to do his will.

But that's not the power that God seeks in this world. He is content only when he rules the whole man, not simply the stubborn will of an individual. Notice Jesus' answer to Pilate's claim of power. "You would have no power unless it had been given you from above" (John 19:11a). In other words, Jesus says that there is no contest. No one is denying Pilate's temporal power. God is not engaged in a struggle of force with the Roman governor.

For God wants a different kind of power over men. He wants men to do his will, not because they have been forced to, but because they are moved by love. God doesn't want soldiers, he wants loving children. The situation is similar to the old story of the contest between the wind and the sun. You remember that in the fable the two engaged in a contest to see which one could get a man to remove his coat. The wind blew and blew, but the man simply pulled his coat tighter around him. But when the warm rays of the sun fell on the man's back he finally removed his coat because he had been warmed clear through. This is God's way of acting and ruling—not by might, but by the warmth of love.

So often we fail to grasp this fact as we recall the lives of the great servants of God. We fail to see that God's power consists of winning men to do his will, regardless of the consequences. When God comes into a man's life, the forces of this world cannot vanquish him. There are two excellent examples of this in the Book of Daniel. Every child knows the story of Daniel and the lions. But the real miracle was not that the lions spared Daniel, but that a man should love God so much that he was willing to face such a test rather than yield to earthly power. The three men who were placed in a fiery furnace illustrate the same truth. They did not know whether they would be rescued or not. But they were willing to die rather than to submit to the power of a heathen ruler.

The crucifixion of Jesus also represents this truth. There is no contest of temporal power between Pilate and Jesus. Pilate wins that contest by default. But the greater struggle is for a man's soul, and here God is victorious, for Jesus accepted the death that awaited him and refused to struggle against it. This is the power of God, a power that does not aim at fighting with the evil forces of life, but that seeks to endure them and ultimately to win the victory through love.

Bishop Hanns Lilje demonstrates this power in his book *The Valley of the Shadow*. He tells how he was imprisoned by the Nazis. God did not prevent Hitler from imprisoning Bishop Lilje. In the prison the monotony did begin to wear down the spirit of this man of God, but he writes: "And yet the consolation of God did not fail." The bishop also tells how on Christmas Day, 1944, he preached to the people in that prison on the text: "The people who walked in darkness have seen a great light." Think of the power that could move a man in prison to speak such words to his fellow prisoners.

This is the power that the Pilates and the Caesars of this world cannot understand. They think in terms of the lash and the whip, of the sword and the gun. They speak of power as the ability to put a man to death or to spare him from that death. God's power is far different. He seeks the whole man. His symbol is the cross, for it was by that cross that goodness conquered and evil was forever defeated. To rule by fear is to rule only a part of a man. To rule by love is to have the willing obedience of a man's whole nature.

But there is another truth that also must not escape us. God not only seeks another type of power but he also works on another time schedule. Jesus hints at that fact when he tells Pilate: " . . . he who delivered me to you has the greater sin" (John 19:11 b.). Jesus thus indicated that there was something beyond Good Friday, a day of reckoning for those who had opposed him. And this fact must not be forgotten. For certainly on Good Friday the power struggle was won by Caesar. Men looking only at the events of that sad day would say that Pilate was stronger than Christ.

No one would say this today, however. Pilate is simply a name mentioned in the Apostles' Creed. Caesar is a term in the history book. But Jesus Christ is known and loved by millions of people. The victory seemed for the moment to be with the powers of darkness, yet the ultimate victory was God's.

In fact, the events of this world might be compared to a motion picture in which the leading characters suffer great difficulties, but finally come to a happy ending. If you stop the picture anywhere along the line, you get a gloomy idea of existence. If you stop at the tragic story of Good Friday, if you stop at Nero's persecution, if you stop at the scene where Hitler did his little dance of triumph over the forces of France, then you would conclude that the powers of this world are stronger than God. But if you wait to see the whole picture, then you will learn that God works on a different time schedule. He's not interested in winning a battle, but in winning the war. He is concerned about ultimate victory; and that always lies in his hands.

Where are the conquerors who exerted their strength and persecuted the church? They have disappeared, one by one. Where are the heretics who threatened to tear the church apart and subvert the Christian witness? They have had their little day and they are gone. In the words of Luther: "The kingdom ours remaineth."

Thus when we look at a situation such as our text portrays, Christ before Pilate, the important thing is that we do not panic. It is so easy to feel, as Elijah did, that the game is lost. It is so easy to take the short, panic-stricken view. But the Christian should know better. Calvary should teach him that the power lies with God and that he will win in the end, despite all that men can do.

God is in no hurry, and that very fact should give us confidence. It's only the man who is afraid that he won't win who gets into a panic and seeks an immediate result. When you know that the victory is yours, you can afford to take your time. And God who won redemption for man through the death of his Son on a cross has all the time in the universe. In the words of Kipling:

The tumult and the shouting dies,
The captains and the kings depart.

But God goes on, always moving toward the victory which is his.

The question of power is a crucial one. But it is not a doubtful question. Man may seem to win, but the true state of affairs is expressed by the closing words of the Lord's Prayer. "For thine is the kingdom, and the power, and the glory, forever and ever, Amen."

Acknowledgments

Scripture quotations are from the Revised Standard Version of the Bible, copyright 1946 and 1952 by the Division of Christian Education of the National Council of Churches.

Page 18. Quotations from *Gilbert Keith Chesterton* by Maisie Ward. Sheed & Ward, Publishers.

Page 25. Quotation from "Lead, kindly light" by John Henry Newman. From *Service Book and Hymnal*, No. 523. By permission of Commission on the Liturgy and Hymnal.

Page 30. Quotation from "Our Christ" by Henry Webb Farrington. From *Masterpieces of Religious Verse*. Reprinted by permission of Harper & Row, Publishers.

Page 37. Quotation from "Invictus" by William Henley. Copyright Macmillan Co., Publishers.

Page 57. Quotation from "No East or West" by John Oxenham. By permission of Theo. Oxenham.

Page 74. Quotation from "The Chief Mourner of Marne." From *The Incredulity of Father Brown* by G. K. Chesterton. By permission of Dodd, Mead & Company, Publishers.

Page 79. Quotation from "Love Lifted Me." From *Hymns of Praise*, Hope Publishing Co. Copyright John T. Benson Jr.

Page 86. Quotation from "Easter Hymn" by A. E. Housman. From *Collected Poems* by A. E. Housman. By permission of Holt, Rinehart and Winston, Inc., Publishers.

Page 89. Quotation from *Valley of the Shadow* by Hanns Lilje. By permission of Fortress Press, Publishers.

Page 92. Quotation from "Recessional" by Rudyard Kipling. By permission of Doubleday & Company, Publishers.

The Author

W. A. Poovey teaches homiletics (preaching) at Wartburg Theological Seminary, Dubuque, Iowa. He is a graduate of Capital University and the Evangelical Lutheran Theological Seminary, Columbus, Ohio, and has a master's degree from Northwestern University. He also has done graduate work at Union Theological Seminary, New York.

In this collection of Lenten sermons Professor Poovey offers meaningful insights gained in 18 years of service in the parish ministry (at Monterey Park, Calif., San Antonio, Texas, and Memphis, Tenn.), in seven years of teaching, and in many years of service on social action committees of The American Lutheran Church.

Professor Poovey is the author of *Your Neighbor's Faith*, *Problems That Plague the Saints*, and other books, and has published several plays.